REVEAL $100 PER DAY

HOW TO MAKE MONEY FROM WRITING ARTICLES EVEN YOU
DON'T KNOW THE TOPICS- LEARN HOW YOU CAN MAKE
MONEY BY WRITING ONLINE AND MAKE $100 PER DAY

WAN MOHD HIRWANI WAN HUSSAIN

REVEAL $ 100 PER DAY

HOW TO MAKE MONEY FROM WRITING ARTICLES EVEN YOU DON'T KNOW THE TOPICS- LEARN HOW YOU CAN MAKE MONEY BY WRITING ONLINE AND MAKE $100 PER DAY

By

WAN MOHD HIRWANI WAN HUSSAIN

INTRODUCTION

This eBook will help and explain about the techniques to generate income writing the articles. If you are looking to have a side income by just writing an article so this eBook is the perfect match for you to start with. There is lot of website that needs writers online and you can easily generated income by writing online. This eBook will give an insight some ideas to help you decide what might work for you to start generating money from writing an article.

Feel free to email me if you need further discussion about the techniques. You can contact me through email at the end of this eBook.

TABLE OF CONTENTS

LEGAL NOTES

Online And Make $100 Per Day have made all reasonable efforts to provide current and accurate information for the readers of this eBook.

Whether because of the general evolution of the Internet, or the unforeseen changes in company policy and editorial submission guidelines, what is stated as fact at the time of this writing, may become outdated or simply inapplicable at a later date. Great effort has been exerted to safeguard the accuracy of this writing. Opinions regarding similar website platforms have been formulated as a result of both personal experience, as well as the well documented experiences of others.

CHAPTER 1. WHY WRITING

Either write something worth reading or do something worth writing.

Benjamin Franklin

The most important things that you should remember when writing an article is to know that it will make money. This is the most important things that you keep in your minds when want to make money from your articles. Writing article is not difficult but it also not so easy. You must passionate and know very well about the topics that you want to write. This will make the writing process easy and will help you to make profit.

There are lots of techniques that can be used to make money from the internet. One of the techniques is to make money using the articles. There are people who make more than $10,000 per month just by writing an article and provide information's for the readers.

It's should be noted here that writing an article is not an easy task. There are people will tell you that writing is the difficult and you should focus on other things. But by writing an article will help you learn and encourage telling others what you know.

What you can do with the articles?

After writing an article, the article can be used...

1. To generate FREE traffic to your blog and website. This will make your website and blog become popular.

2. Getting traffic by sending and promoting affiliate links. (Generate more income for you every month).

3. Make money from the Google Adsense. Google Adsense is one of the popular making money on the internet. There are many people generate money using this ways.

4. You can combine the entire article to create an e-Book that can be sold through online. This will multiply your income. You can also sell resell rights of this book to the customers.

5. You can sell the article to the corporate organizations or small medium enterprise (SME). There are many corporate organization and SME that required fresh and new contents for their website.

6. You can become article ghostwriter or freelancer article writer. There are many freelance website that need good writers. You can search it at the internet.

7. You can also make your article become viral and become famous. This will make you become popular and well known author.

The internet provides you will the information at your fingertips. It is called as the "information highway". Everyday there are many people that surfing the internet to find information and to learn new knowledge.

It is your jobs to provide reliable and good information about the certain topics. The people will pay you money if you can provide them with the information that you needs.

When writing an article you must forget about everything that you learn in the class and please write it with your own way and technique.

Here is the advice for you when writing an article:

a) Please don't use the big words and you can just simply your words. This will make the reader understand about the topics and can learn it easily.

b) Please don't become boring writer. The people will read your article online and always make them become feel "alive" when reading your article.

c) Always be yourself. Don't try to duplicate other writer and be yourself. This will make you unique and the people will know about your style of writing.

d) Keep the contents fresh and new. You must know about the topics very well and describe it in a very simple term that the people will understand. In order to achieve this, you must always reading and reading every day. Through reading will help you find new information and will improve your article skills.

I read and walked for miles at night along the beach, writing bad blank verse and searching endlessly for someone wonderful who would step out of the darkness and change my life. It never crossed my mind that that person could be me.

Anna Quindlen

CHAPTER 2. FINDING YOUR TOPICS

All good writing is swimming under water and holding your breath.

F. Scott Fitzgerald

The most important things before writing an article are to find and know about your topics. There are many techniques that you can be used to find topics for your articles. By finding the topics you will attract the customers and much easier for you to tell others about your expertise. This section will describe about the topics or information that you can used to write your article.

Before you start findings the topics for your article, you must do this exercise which is..

a) Find a place that FREE from any distractions.
   This can be done by switching any electronic devices that you own and focus on the topics that come to your mind.

b) Note Taking process

At this stage you will capture any ideas that come to your minds. This is the note taking process. You can use any tools or devices that you fell can help you in note taking. There are many tools such as note pad, Evernote and Google Drive that can be used to capture any new ideas that can be used in writing new article. By using online tools, you can store it online and accessed it anytime that you want. This will help you more efficient and effective in managing time.

c) Manage your time- only 30 minutes brainstorming process.

You must set up your time to 30 minutes to come out with a new idea nor more than that. This will you become productive and pressure to getting the work to be done. After 30 minutes you can analyzed what you have achieved. By doing this exercise regularly you can train and stay motivated when doing and finishing a job.

d) Asking yourself

This is the last stage that you must do in order to get ideas for your article. By asking yourself you will get what you want to write and tell the readers. Asking the question will trigger your mind to learn and know about the new information that is valuable for your readers. You must come out with at least 30 questions from the topics that you want to write.

Here are the other techniques that you can use to find topics for your articles;

1. From your mentee/mentor
2. From your partner
3. From current event
4. From Your parents

5. From Your friends

6. From your child

7. Watching a news

8. A movie

9. Social media friends

When writing a Novel a Writer should create living people; people not characters. A character is a caricature.

Ernest Hemingway

CHAPTER 3. TURNING YOUR ARTICLE INTO INCOME

Learn as much by writing as by reading.

Lord Acton

When writing an article you must know that the people want the information fast and they also want to learn it quickly as possible. Most of the readers will look for the shortcut way to learn and start applying the new knowledge that they gain. With this in mind, they will not want fluff information and want the information that easy to understand.

When writing an article always knows that this article will help you generate income and the people will pay you money of you has information that they want.

When writing an article you must stay focused on the topics and provide useful information for the reader. You must educate the readers.

Quality of the articles is the most important things and always does the research about the topics and writes the articles based in your understanding.

Provide them with the information but not too much because this will make them know about the topics and don't want to subscribe into your ideas or article anymore.

Then you must use the search engine to make you penetrate the search engine. You can use Google, Bing or Yahoo and get the first spot at the search engine. This is the way you can monetize your income from the article. By owning top spot at the search engine will make you sell your product or services much easier.

Make money from Blogging

You can also make money from your article by blogging. There are many sites that will pay you to blog.

Here is the site:

Squidoo	http://www.squidoo.com/
Hubpages	http://hubpages.com/
Helium	https://www.helium.c

	om/
Epinions	http://www.epinions.com/
Fiverr	https://www.fiverr.com/
Digital Journal	http://www.digitaljournal.com
About	http://experts.about.c

	om/
Blogging	http://blogging.org/
Xomba	http://www.xomba.com/
Wizzley	https://wizzley.com/
Sponsored Reviews	http://www.sponsoredreviews.com/

Info Barrel	http://www.infobarrel.com/
Snipsly	http://snipsly.com/
Text Broker	https://www.textbroker.com/
Developer Tutorials	http://www.developertutorials.com/

World Start	http://www.worldstart.com/
Spyre studios	http://spyrestudios.com/
Ecommer insiders	http://ecommerceinsiders.com/
Back 2 college	http://www.back2college.com/guide.htm

The Tech Labz	http://www.thetechlabz.com/
Ceramics	http://ceramics.org/
Change Agent	http://changeagent.nelrc.org/
Strecher	http://www.stretcher.com/

Dropzone	http://www.dropzone.com/
Metroparent	www.metroparent.com
Theme Forest	http://themeforest.net/
A Fine Parent	http://afineparent.com/

Smashing Magazine	http://www.smashingmagazine.com/
Funds For Writers	http://www.fundsforwriters.com/

I feel like I'm too busy writing history to read it.

Kanye West

CHAPTER 4. TOOLS TO WRITE ARTICLES

There are many tools that you can used to writing your article and improve your productivity. Using this tool will help you manage your time and spend your time in marketing your articles for profit.

This is the must have tools that you need in order to become a good and successful writers.

Wordstream	http://www.wordstream.com/
Grammarly	https://www.grammarl

	y.com/
Copyscape	http://www.copyscape.com/
Fotolia	https://us.fotolia.com/
Write or Die	http://writeordie.com/
Dictionary	http://www.tfd.com/

Tip my tongue	http://chir.ag/projects/tip-of-my-tongue/
Text to Speech	http://free-translation.imtranslator.net/speech.asp
Online diary	https://penzu.com/
Word Counter	http://www.wordcounte

	r.com/
Creativity portal	http://www.creativity-portal.com/prompts/imagination.prompt.html
Zen writer	http://www.beenokle.com/zenwriter.html
Byword	http://bywordapp.com/
Readability	https://readability.com/

Stay focused	Search at google chrome
Article writer tool	http://articlerewritertool.com/
Portent	http://www.portent.com/tools/title-maker
Buzzsumo	http://buzzsumo.com/

Quora	http://www.quora.com/
Trello	https://trello.com/
Evernote	https://evernote.com/
Todoist	https://en.todoist.com/
Wunderlist	https://www.wunderlist.com/

Dropbox	https://www.dropbox.com/
Content Idea Generator	http://www.contentideagenerator.com/
Google Keyword Planner	https://adwords.google.com/KeywordPlanner
Keyword tool	http://keywordtool.io/

Yoast wordpress plugin	https://yoast.com/wordpress/plugins/seo/
Google trends	https://www.google.com/trends/
Egg timer	http://e.ggtimer.com/
Toggle	https://www.toggl.com/
Hemingway	http://www.hemingway

	app.com/
Desk	http://desk.pm/

You can also use the social media as the way to generate ideas and get new information.

There are many social media that available in the internet as using the social media will help in you in improving the quality of the articles.

Linked in	https://www.linkedin.com/nhome/
Facebook	http://www.facebook.com
Twitter	https://twitter.com/
Hubspot	http://www.hubspot.com/blog-topic-generator
Tagged	http://www.tagged.com/

Meetme	http://www.meetme.com/
Ning	http://www.ning.com/
Bebo	http://www.bebo.com/

Writing is an exploration. You start

from nothing and learn as you go.

E. L. Doctorow

CHAPTER 5: WHAT YOU SHOULD KNOW ABOUT "GOOD" ARTICLE

Writing articles is the most difficult task and the articles will provides the information and will help in generating new knowledge for the readers. Articles also can be used to tell the story

In order to write good article there are a few techniques that can be used which is the article must be maintain around 1 to 3 % percent of keyword density.

There are many examples that you can used to create your first article. There are also a website resources that you can used such as ezine articles, article city and many more. This site will help you to learn and creating your first article.

This section will analyze and provides information how to develop a good article that can engage with the customers.

There are 8 steps that you can used to write an article which is:

a) You must start somewhere

This is important because in writing an article you must start from somewhere not waiting for the perfect conditions.

"I was told just to write. My heart would do the rest and I would learn professional tips along the way... My writing pathway is now clear and moves forward ... into the future."

- Sandy Giles

b) Find inspiration

In order for you to write you must find the inspiration that will inspire you to write and keep motivated. Always write something that you interested most. This will help you not bored with the topics.

"'C'mon, can't you write a bit more?' – my partner used to say this to me and it ultimately helped me to overcome procrastination :-)"

- Frederik Kreijmborg

c) Title of your article

You must have the title of your article. The title must be attractive to attract the readers to read your articles.

d) Offer solution

The article must provide information and give the solutions for whatever problem. This is important because the readers want to get solutions that you have outlined for them.

e) Keep it concise

You must also keep the information in your article concise and precise. Do not bluff your reader with the information that is not correct.

f) Create an outline

Before writing an article you must first outline the content and paragraph that you need to write. This will help you maintain the flow of the article and make you readers understand about your topics.

g) Review your article

You also must review your article before submission process. Always look for any grammar error that occurs. Then you also must familiar yourself with the editorial guidelines that required.

h) Submit your article

The last process is the submission process. Before submit you must know the requirement of the journal. Always contact the editor if you have any problem regarding the submission process.

"First, think about the problem your readers want to solve. Second, think about at least 6 ways the problem could be solved. Do the research. Third, think some more about the several ways there are to meet the reader's needs. Fourth, sleep on it. Fifth, start writing with excitement and enthusiasm. Sixth, put it away and then do the editing tomorrow. Seventh. Done!"

Terrance L. Weber

CHAPTER 6.
Make Money Writing Articles: Which Topics Are The Best?

If you want to writing article for money you must know what the topics that interested the readers are:

a) Finance
b) Health
c) Parenting
d) Debt
e) Weight Loss
f) Language
g) Making Money online
h) Games
i) New Gadgets & Technology
j) Real Estate
k) Managing Money

I) Investment

This is the example of the topics that you can use to write an article. You can also search the forum to find information about the topics that people keep asking. This will provide you with the information for your new articles.

You can also start writing that you love to. For example you can write article on hobby or travel holidays that you have been.

Writing and finding a topic is a crucial part in article development process. You must know what are the people looking to and address the solution for that matter.   By expanding you knowledge that you will be able to write on many topics you can increase the chance to make money and sell the article to others.   The people will pay for the quality of the article.

As a conclusion, you must understand and write about the topics that interested the people. This is important for the writer that wants to make money online.

CHAPTER 7.
Conclusion

(1) Keep it simple, (2) less is more, and (3) do it now."

Jeff Herring

As the conclusion, writing an article is a big business, there are many people that generated lot of money by writing an article for the organization, company and people. You must be patience and try establish your networking in writing. This will make people know about you and establish your creditability as an expert in the fields.

"Come back to the article in a few months to see how it is performing … A great article evolves over time."

Scott Bateman

CHAPTER 10.

Dr Wan Mohd Hirwani Wan Hussain
wmhwh@ukm.edu.my

I am an enthusiastic and professional, who enjoys being part of, as well as leading, a successful and productive team. I am quick to grasp new ideas and concepts, and to develop innovative and creative solutions to problems. I am able to work well on my own initiative and can demonstrate the high levels of motivation required to meet the tightest of deadlines. Even under significant pressure, I possess a strong ability to perform effectively.

Dr Wan Mohd Hirwani Wan Hussain Ph.D is a university researcher at Graduate School of Business, UKM and internet marketing entrepreneur. He has been involved in internet marketing since 2006 and have many product in varies in e-book and mobile application. He has published numerous articles in international conference and journal publication. Specialties: Internet Marketing, Search Marketing, eCommerce, Search Engine Optimization, SEO, Search Engine Marketing, SEM, Mobile Marketing, Sponsored Advertising.

Having over 8 years' experience in internet marketing, search engine marketing (SEM), search engine optimization (SEO), business development, product, service and internet marketing, he knows how to cost-effectively bring products and services to the internet market place. He has consulted with hundreds of customers about their business, ecommerce and internet solutions, helping them ensure a return on their technology investment.

Google analytics, Google adwords, Facebook advertising, Twitter, Pinterest, Linkedin, Google+.

OTHER BOOKS BY (AUTHOR)

Please check my other e-book.

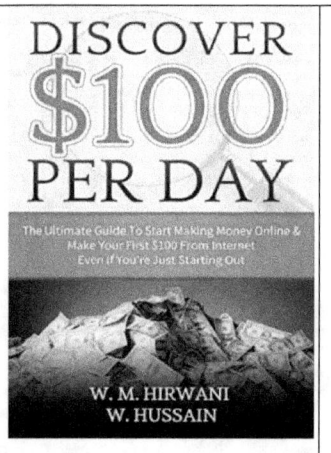	http://www.amazon.com/DISCO VER-ULTIMATE-MAKING-ONLINE-INTERNET-ebook/dp/B00K0LBHS8/ref=sr_1 _2?s=digital-text&ie=UTF8&qid=1435036865 &sr=1-2&keywords=100+per+day
	http://www.amazon.com/Student-Entrepreneurship-Innovation--Business-Strategy-ebook/dp/B00TESIQK0/ref=sr_1 _3?s=digital-text&ie=UTF8&qid=1435036974 &sr=1-3&keywords=student+entrepreneurship
	http://www.amazon.com/DEBT-FAST--MONEY--QUICKEST-SIMPLEST-

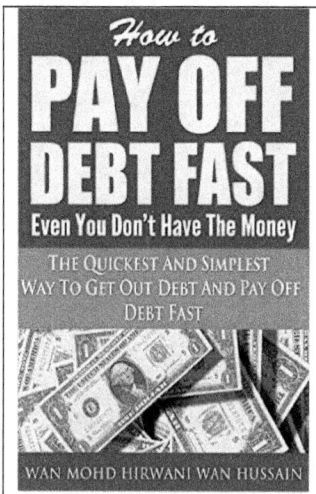

ebook/dp/B013FJE6PM/ref=asa
p_bc?ie=UTF8

www.ingramcontent.com/pod-product-compliance
Lightning Source LLC
Chambersburg PA
CBHW062019280526
45787CB00005B/2171